A Pageant

FOR EVERY

Addiction

POEMS BY

Thomas Fink

AND

Maya Mason

MARSH HAWK

2020

D1069307

First Edition
1   3   5   7   9   10   8   6   4   2
Printed in the USA

Marsh Hawk Press books are published by Poetry Mailing List, Inc.,
a not-for-profit corporation under section 501 (c) 3 United States Internal Revenue Code.

Cover painting © Maya D. Mason and Thomas Fink,
"A Pageant for Every Addiction," oil on canvas, 2019.

Book design by Heather Wood
www.HeatherWoodBooks.com

The text is set in Utopia.

Library of Congress Cataloging-in-Publication Data
Fink, Thomas, 1954– and Maya D. Mason, 1993–
[Poems. Selections]
A Pageant for Every Addiction / Thomas Fink and Maya D. Mason. – First Edition.
Pages; cm.
Includes bibliographical references.
ISBN 13: 9780996991209 (pbk.) — ISBN 10: 0996991209 (pbk.)
I. Title   PS   201

 Marsh
Hawk
Press

Marsh Hawk Press
P.O. Box 206
East Rockaway, New York 11518-0206
www.marshhawkpress.org

CONTENTS

A
Pageant
FOR EVERY
Addiction

FIRST DATE QUESTIONS

I found a dime
in the parking lot;
should I hand it over
to the cops? Has life

been better since you left the womb?
If you hit the jackpot, what

chunk would you invest?
Do you need to be rich to live
in your birthplace?

Can you be forthright
about the quality
of your native soil?
Aren't there

different ways to be uninteresting?
I've only tried a handful. Do

you trust people who spell
creatively? Why
would anyone hang pictures

of strangers throughout
their house? Can
a picture spit
on you when

it's talking? How much weight
do you shed when you sneeze? If

you got a thin
moon slice,
would you complain
to the manager? Aren't

those birds too chubby to be perching
in a tree? How did they get up

there? Have you ever
seen a 200 pound
man who thought he was

a butterfly?
A caterpillar
who thought
he was
a moustache?

Would you invest
in a factory that makes
shoelaces too
short? Do you

pause to sniff workout socks?
Do you hear a fly buzz when you

haven't showered? What
color is nothing? Can
terriers imagine peace

in the Middle East?
Is a dog self-
conscious about
being the only

family member with a tail? Don't
you just hate when you reach the zoo,

and the zebras have been sent
out for cleaning? Is the zoo
rent-free for the tenants?

Do wild beasts
ever let
their guard down
enough to fall

asleep? Why did they teach preschoolers
about hibernation before we

had a glimpse at human
weirdness? If you are a goat's
father, are you still a

father?
My concept
of cheese
is very
American.

Sanitized. And yours?
Would you like some
of this delicious
ham? Has our violated

ecosphere induced you to abandon
3 of your 5 favorite dishes?

Do you mind when delectable food
comes in a jar, and you have
to cut up a hand

to get out every
last drop of
it? Do they
make smaller

sushi for children's mouths? Could
a chemist be a lousy cook?

Can vegetables have
STDs?
If crabapples are

the sole available
fruit, can you
enjoy them?
Do our facial

features take up enough
room on our faces? How do all

the organs stay in place
and not fall out of the anus?
Tell me what it's like to have

your teeth.
Where is
having
teeth a
status

symbol? Why
wear glasses
if you don't
have eyes?

Why am I repulsed by people
with small teeth? It's not a

life-choice but feels
like one. Is the Pope
circumcised? How do I

slip past
someone envious
of my nose? Ever
blown your nose into

a headwind? Can you be allergic
to your own tears? If Hitler had

a regular person moustache,
would moustaches be verboten?
Is being German fun?

Do Anselm Kiefer's
grisly hues and
char reel
out your ancestors'

angst? Yes, a painter. Noted
enough for you to have.... Oh,

you're half Jewish?
When did they get here?
Are you an American

today?
Can you
see the
beauty in
abandoned

spaces? Do you
think you'll
ever lose
your native accent?

And could you conceivably find it
again? Everyone walks through the

same air, so why
can't they swim in the same
water? Why aren't there

competitions for things
that are easy? Do you
ever want to
start a family

out of boredom? What's your take on eager
prospective egg donors?

Can vegans eat egg
plant? Do fetuses in
utero scream? Can a

pregnant woman
drive "solo" in the
HOV
lane? How fat

does a child have to be not to require
a car seat? If you had a baby with

crummy facial features,
could you still deem it loveable?
Are you self-conscious

about
dogs and
babies
when
they don't

reciprocate
your affection?
What do you
do if you never

wished to parent, but longed to be
a grandparent? Want some grand

children? Who's hiding in
those clouds overhead?
Do all insects die

in the winter or do
they go south?
I hate to think of
worms eating my

dog's eyes; is that love?
How long do medical offices

keep your records after
you expire? When
you have an unwanted thought,

do you screech not
to hear? What's your
PR for
epiphanies in a

single day? Do you wash your
hands after writing a poem?

Can you get an STD
from kissing the Blarney Stone?
What would you do if a policeman

declared your
art
illegal?
Do we call
it pedo

philia if a child
pinches another
child? Do your hands
feel dirty in

an unfamiliar place? How
do you feel when bare arms

brush yours in the subway?
Have people in New
York grown taller in

the last 10
years? How
do you not
bleed? Your t-

shirt prays for me; should I
be happy? Why are the

precise people for whom
shirts were invented not
wearing shirts? Is an

action immoral
if no one can
watch? Why
would a suit

of armor have nipples?
If Caravaggio had

electric light, would
tenebrism exist?
Could you imagine a world

where
everything
is printed
on rose-
colored
paper?

Is that a hotel
or does everybody
have the same
curtains? Can trees

be afraid of heights? Does
it bother you that your eyes are so

far from the ground? Have poppy
seeds dominated your
equilibrium?

Why do they keep
inventing these
new ancient
grains? Can

you rent space on someone's
body to tattoo? May I

have a word with your
unconscious? Can
I borrow your silk rhetoric

for my next slob
interview? Were
you ever small
enough to fit

into a teacup? Ever feel
like a trick-pony that couldn't

negotiate the jump?
Is there a minimum
age requirement for

a nursing home?
If I have a heart
attack, is there a
doctor in the parking

lot? Which is more spectacular:
two voices speaking through

one mouth or one
voice through two
mouths?

GRAY BUS

Oh, what your mother looks like. My shadow
was walking faster than me.
The zip code was in disrepute. Somebody had to
fix it. They kept filling the air with

wads of words, a gray bus
that takes you to a change

of sheen. Cures more lives than death.
We have it now, don't we? Do
I take all the girls there?

Mirror

I don't look

in my eyes much because
I find reproach
there. She acts like singing
is an act of violence.

I'm going to hug you now.

I'm Very Beautiful Today

I
have an enchanting
smile.

The body
is an amazing
tool.

For a year
there was a different date
every day.

Lately, walls
are screaming,
shrinking.

Memories
make good rags.

Corporate Angel

Don't push anything with this girl.
She's the Senior Vice President of blah blah blah blah.
She's so busy and so snobby, but she loves me.
This angelic type of—
happy, smiling.

I don't think her teeth are yellow.
Everyone's like—
where are you going this weekend?

My dollhouse happens to be a Colonial.
I'm moving Saturday.

I Don't Want to See Her Damaged So I'll Buy a New Pair of Glasses and Draw Her a New Face

I swear this was when she was drenched.

Think she's had
like 5 jobs.

Sucks.
It was like

So—
I don't know—

Alzheimer's.
We'll try to be right

behind you. You can
only be a friend when

something like that . . .
I'd have to

do everything in my power
to

stop you; I'd have to
save the world.

We were holding her
arm: that's

how bad.
"Oh my god,"

I said,
"You're

so cool, you're
so pretty, you're so

fun how can you
not see?"

Kind of like:
whoa! Lost.

I will be so
upset; I will be

so disappointed.
I need my

monkey
to comfort me.

You're Morally Inferior If

you clomp audibly
on wood floors, you
wear down heels
within four months,

you lust after ordinary
delicacies, a single
window "graces"
your dwelling,

you fail to shower
thoroughly before kissing,
you exceed the one-
pet rule,

you grew large
breasts during early
puberty (or as a middle-
aged male),

you keep
fingernails long—
rendering hands useless,
you include tax

while calculating tip,
you don't offer to shovel
your host's snowy driveway,
you do nothing about

your weak chin,
you woke up today
after I did,
you wear summertime

pants that accent
egregious girth,
your parents bolloxed
your childhood dental

care, you're 33
and can't drive,
your cooking commits
olfactory offense, you

buy two of the same
necklace, you're too
sentimental to kill
a mere mouse.

You reuse
plastic silverware.
You don't anticipate
my tacit needs.

I'm Bothering You So Go Away

It has
come to our attention
that you have
come to our attention,
due to a
system error.

Please
rectify this
at once
by removing yourself
from our doorstep,
our desktop.

You and your
legion of no ones,
who lack, could
distract us unconscionably from our crucial mission.

Warning:
do not expect a
thank-you
for a reflex that should be

automatic.

WEIGHTLIFTER'S GHETTO

Oatmealers aren't immune
to the fate of an unlucky pedestrian,
struck in the prime
by inexplicable death.

The bulk of a generation
tumbling into debt to keep
their gym affiliation.

They want to muscle in
forever
more, but

injustice may trespass.

Some reside in vehicular domiciles
to defray the expense of marching
on a treadmill.

THRIFT

Dirty moonlight makes
this a bad night
for sightseeing.

I can teach you how to consume an apple.
You're missing the meat of it.

BUMPER CROP

Proud legal guardian of a spectacular
crack addict.

Incontinent idiot in a
hurry.

Violent patriarchal
psychopath on board.

Marriage:
seemed like a good
idea at the time.

Dyslexic
no broad.

We hate
that our grandparents are
not.

Glad you can
read, but do you
vote?

Illiteracy
got me into college.

Color-
blind driver on
board.

Patron of the Museum
of Unnatural Mysteries.

My hybrid
will take me to heaven;

your guzzling
monstrosity will speed you to hell.

My taxes
pay for your children's
adequate schooling.

Glad you vote, but
can you read?

People
don't count. Machines
count.

I can't afford to
live another
70 years.

Caution: makes wild
left assumptions.

Keep your politics
on the inside (of
the car).

My other car
is a sherpa.

He died.
For.

In memory of a forgotten
crossing guard.

For your sins.

Try not to forget the true
meaning of Ground
Hog's Day.

Don't live too
simply, or many
could be ejected from their jobs.

Your voices behind
the veal mutter.

I brake for
litigious-
looking motorists.

I'm not a
big fan of yours,
because you
don't know who
I am.

You're trailing an ego
that would blow smoke in anyone's
mug.

Unless you're illiterate,
don't wash my windshield.

Rickety bicycles,
back off.

FBI informant
in trunk.

Slightly embalmed
corpse in the back seat.

Don't touch my
motherfucking pizza.

Animals are
edible, too.

Yes, I did kill
the plants,
but much
will be different from here
on in.

Are you going to eat that?

Honk if you brushed all
your teeth today.

Please refrain from tailgating
unless you are unbearably attractive.

Bumper stickers are for
bottom feeders.

Almost Magnificent

I didn't know that you didn't know.
We each brought our own dinner,
and I did the cooking.
But she'd kept every cookbook.

Almost magnificent red clam sauce.
And this I think an improvement
over sumptuous but indigestible.

The hours of indigestion gluttony
invited. A big fat
ice cream ring.
My first furniture casualty.

Her son very often forgets to give me arms.

He would not mind selling his
paintings, but would not permit them
to be exhibited. The price is a bit
more than I care to be paying.

The family kept congratulating
themselves; they may have
achieved a telephone. And leave me
with nothing but my own unstimulating company.

Nothing New Or Even Interesting

I never knew there was so much god
damned fish floating around. Since I read
of no mishaps on Sunday, I will assume
that you arrived as scheduled and in

approximately the same state of good
health I've kept you in these past many
months—you lucky girl! Stagnant

since you've been foraging. Though colliding
with a wonderful relic built with the purpose of
making hammers. Highly speculative infant
enterprises stir no pungent broth in me.

And the big ones are no bargains, either.
This is the crummiest town of its size
and weight. And I doubt we'll get rich

on the quantities they'll seek.
Actually, therefore, I'm no closer to the
solution now than I was when commissioned
in the Quartermaster Corps from OCS for

express purpose of tending to piers,
except that I'm fast coming to accept
the dismal thought of "honest and faithful

service." Undaunted, but lightly
dented, I'll go on. And for free, too.
Just go right on thinking I'll be back. Ever
the conscientious schmo, I can't pass up a

spot on the roadmap I didn't know
existed. Rambling I remain. I wish you were
here—either with me or instead of me.

You are constantly in these thoughts; there isn't
a decent movie in tow. Eyes bugged out
from all that television. I hope you are still bored.
Tucked into your Greenville foxhole with

the AM plugged in. Just retribution in this
exile. And while on the subject of romance,
I'll assume that you do eat my letters.

HOMEMAKING

Too lazy to do it.

The dog makes many artistic
contributions; we hope
he discovers minimalism.
Do some folks spend 10 hours licking

the linoleum spotless?
Scrubbing toilets—on the to-
do list every four
months. No barbecues, please:

the grille takes
a full sitcom
to clean.
Only the finest
paper plates from Paris.
Just learned to turn on his own

oven. After seven years.

From 1950 With Love

1

Milady chooses many comfortable nights
of profound sleeping.

Buttoned simply for warmth, summer
dancing affairs.
Novelty pockets, decidedly
feminine. If

she wants to carry the whims of
fashion that far,
a fellow needn't
perturb himself. Of course,

Susie is a tad
young for college,
though the exact location of the button is

still visible.

It's just that the cocoon
is putting on the right eyes
to match her gown of yellow
dairy. Softly sweeping
bodices form the horseshoe

centerpiece.
The only thing designers are unanimous about
is that natural shoulder

line and efficient
skirts seem
the brightest touch

in the spring forecast.
Street-length dress or mint-
green suit for the minor
lights? Junior train
for a double-ringed ceremony?
Fingertip veil.

The rest is up
to your figure.
And whether you figure you're up to
making practical adjustments that are

less yummy than what's customary.
The couple will
make their domicile on a DIY
farm in Coffin's Grove.

2

Music
was provided by white flowers with
tailored sleeves under
white satin elbow
crepe. Hat of flowers

with jewel accents
escorted down the
isle of greens and lifted
tapers toward the cluster heirloom

orchid in a
silver bon-bon dish garnished
in pressure-cooked Quaker
cloth. At pre-
nuptial courtesies, white lynx
collar honored.

Our silent butler wore
a white lace ballerina gown
with scalloped effervescence, a veil
of imported English net with rhinestone-

starred headpiece while
proffering the bride-elect's whistling
tea to our lazy daisy
toastmaster, as the angel
trio, hummel figures in chiffon

negligee fashioned with unpressed pleats, long

sleeves tapering to points over
green-striped, peach-tinted
wrists, lavish
refreshment table.

Jonquil blossom time.
Guests included
husband.
The full circular back panel
ended in court,

as tiny pink
sweethearts on the mirror
accented the bridge
salad, flower and animal game.

3

When the king's daughters met
Thursday for dessert, one carried
yellow and white
carnations. Each
knew (intuitively)

that she must be a woman
capable of shouldering three jobs.

The group voted
$2
to the cancer
fund. "For if we make this community
perfect, then what could Communism

have to sell?"
Our esteemed

needlecraft book is festooned with
hobby and gift concepts,
and whatever lovely
embroidery your unbounded fancy
can conceive.

THE IDEAL

In 1307, a Roman
emperor outlawed ostentatious

displays of opulence. That lion's balls
look pretty decadent to me. Why
would a suit of armor have

nipples if it weren't made
of chocolate? The body
ideal is sculpted

only in the marble
imagination of a Herculean pansexual.

BREATHTAKINGLY DISHONEST

She's smelling a shrink.
He shrinks into a white wall.

"The dead expect me to be
on call for life."

A few life-deranging sentences.

Every booth is wire-tapped.

REMAINS

We wished her a long,
fruitful engagement
though she was not dressed
for such an announcement.

"Communication
is the answer and
the question."

Opaque registry instructions.

Oh, and the engagement
was posthumous.
Much time horizontal.

Did They Dismiss School When Marilyn

Monroe died?
It was summertime.

The studio did
everything it could to push
the baby out.

She had, they felt,
dropped out of the sky.
A void appears
in the coffee.

Is yawning archival?

You can't return a dress after
you've cried in it.

MAKE MONEY, READ GOOD BOOKS, DON'T SHIT IN YOUR PANTS

Eat while you can.
Without language, all
the bears get up at the same

time in the morning and look
for breakfast. If you don't see
your food, you can't taste it.

Ask 'em for money while
still young enough
to misuse it. Purchase

the latest technologies
to dodge the scorn of the Amish.
Don't arrive at a function

before your hair has dried.
Avoid hot-button
issues like dinosaurs

at dinner parties to keep from
miffing Evangelicals.
Don't try to name

the artist who painted the sky.
With those who act shy,
you're confident, so why

shy away from the gregarious?
Can't marry rich if
you don't know Rich.

There's someone "out there"
for you. Statistically speaking,
likely dead. May
not wish to procreate,

though one can change their mind.
Contemplating parenthood?
Learn how to hide

cookies. Unlike sunflowers,
kids don't raise
themselves. Love all

your children equally
and your husband even

less. If you
don't like

someone, don't
give birth

to them. If you're
alone on Saturday

nights, try
divorce. Lie

copiously to cultivate
lasting friendships.

Don't throw
anyone a rope

made of dental
floss. Why

apply lipstick
to impress a canine?

If you spend more
than 33 seconds

a day thinking
about appearance,

you may qualify
for health insurance.

Going for a walk?
Wear shoes.

Befriend not
one who lacks

deodorant.
Have the fortitude

to overlook
olfactory mishaps.

Buy real
estate on credit
if you lack means.

Expecting more from
a car—new,

used—than you would
from a person is

idiotic. Don't be
the kind who'd be burned
at the Salem trials.

Try your best to
be a good

restaurant. Try
anything once

except a red
car, which jacks

up insurance.
Want to paint

all black
canvases? Invest

covertly in dark
blue. Take a

nanosecond
to smell fish

gizzards. The more underwear,
the less need to launder.

Only sunbathe nude
if you've stolen the neighbors'
binoculars. No one

feels bad for animals,
even though they're always
scraping by—often

in expensive neighborhoods—
and have made no provisions
for retirement. Birds know

much more than we
do about what's
happening under water.

Trees grow birds.
Why don't we cut down
all the trees so we don't

have so many leaves
to deal with? Since I close
all the windows each

morning, it really doesn't
get too dirty.
Schedule midday naps:

everything happening in slumber
is far more scintillating than
daytime events. Please

don't croak until you've
organized your paperwork. No
death tax in Florida.

Six months and one
day. I think you're
gonna be Jewish in your old

age. Humans are made
of water but rarely evaporate.
It's too hard to be inevitable.

CRACKS IN A ROAD

He was a living
person until

he died. A dog
named for the wind.

Miles between
the teeth.

(Original paperwork illegible.)

To the mausoleum.
To get directions.

Thanks, Mary

Times are gruff.

The Virgin lent
her turkey baster.

After birthing triplets in the Laundromat,

one selects
two, at most.

Thanks, Mary.

When you rip the cord out of the wall,
the machine

continues.

EVERYONE GETS

only an inch in Manhattan,

so when Aunt discovered a ridiculous
trick to shed 100 lbs. in 27

minutes, Nephew and Niece
brought up the rebound

effect.

Sean and Dawn

Does a whale
have possessions
that it keeps in the same place?
Sean moved into the bottom

and pays rent,
but his goal is to buy
that house.
Dawn would love it.

I attempted to do
her hair one day.

Substitute Fossil

We swerve
today—from the germs of a statue—
synthesizing a bend as
well as a beckoning,

defying
repercussions of chastity. For I swim
before you and almighty
gold the same swollen

oat. Our
folksingers psychoanalyze crash pads.
The wheel is very different.
No? Our foreman holds

in his motel
the powder to admonish all flakes
of hubris pie and all fumes
of hankypanky. And

yet the same
evolutionary briefs are still issued around
the glockenspiel. Relief
comes not from a

concubine's
freedom but from the hand soap of
genetics. We dare not forge
the hair first. Let

the worm
grow forth from this tomb. To fringe
and foam alike, that the touch
of bureaucracy has been

pressed to a
new gene—torn in this center, hampered
by woe, disciples of a hardy
birthrate plunge,

prostrated by
our aching stage—unwillingly witless. Let
every nostril blow, and we shall
spray any lice, bare any

bumpkin,
melt any hardware, pose with any felon
to assure the success of
charismatic librarians.

This much
we plod. And more. To those old almonds,
whose cultural spittoon ornaments
we shed, we plinth the lullaby

and plough
the lunatic of falsetto frissons. Ignited,
there is little we cannot chew
in a hotbed of cooperative

vertebrae.
Derided, there is little we can rue, for we dare
not mute a power champagne
odyssey and spoof.

To those new
stay-at-homes whom we weld into the ransoms
of the freed, we plead our wire
that one fossil of combat

shall not have
been pierced astray merely to be relaced by a far
more irrelevant udder. Find them
smugly sporting their own

freeway and
redden the paste for those who ghoulishly sought
practicality by riding the backbone
of time. To those perfectionists

in the hymnals
and vintages, half the glow struggling to break in
bongos for the matador misogynist,
we plough our best eggheads

to hear them
heap themselves for what perjury is re-queered.
Not because the commuters may
be driving it, but because

we seek
their candid vowels. If a free sock cannot help
the many who are at war, it cannot
save those who are ridiculed

by peace.
To our sit-in reruns, souvenir of our borehole,
we offer a special plight to convict
our glad workhorses into gold

deficits—in
a new alphabet for potpourri to assume
maneaters of grammar castrate
the chairmen of prattle, but

this pitiful
rhapsody of hormones cannot become the priest
of hostile practitioners. Let all our
neurotics know that we shall

joust with them
to oppose agony. And let every prankster
know that this heretic tends to remain
the bane of its own houseplant.

To that worship
assessor of spaceship statisticians the unnecessary
necessities, our last best horsewhip in
an argument where the intellects

of wardrobe
have far outpaced wholesome intake of raw
peanut, we renew our playbill to
prevent it from becoming

merely a foundry
for indignation—to strengthen its shingle and to
enlarge the armada in which its
yacht may roam. Finally,

to those navigators
who would make themselves our airplane, we offer
not a ploy but a reservation: that both
sidewalks begin a new quintet

for pleasantry
before the darling detective leaked by scoopfuls
engulf all humor in plain or occidental
seminary determination. We

dare not thump
them with weather. For only when our armchairs
are suffused beyond downgrade can
we be certain beyond downpour

that they will
endure. But neither can two gritty, putrid grudge
exigencies take a comma from our
pressed corruption, both

siestas overburdened
by the cough of modern weekdays, both ripely
swarmed by a deadly attic, yet each
retching to ambush that

uncertified balloon
of testimony that stays the handcuff of an unkind
final warp. So let us bargain for a new
remunerating clairvoyance, not

a silk web,
sinus always subsidized with prophylactic. Let
us never negotiate felicity. But let us
never feast to negate.

Let both sods
implore probability of union instead of labor
divisions. Let both side-dishes
farm syrupy protests against

the infection. Beware
a dissolute contrition. Yet napkins provoke
wanderings. Together let us
export the stores, conquer

the desserts,
trap the ocean. And let the confessed retain their
fee. And if a breach of corporations
may hack the juggling of

scorpions,
let us join in peach reserves. But let us bargain. In
your hoops, my criminals will rust a final
succulence. Now the tourniquet

sums up
a cow to butter the breadbox, juicing tribal litigation,
a strut against curdled entities. Can we
force against these entropies

a grunting
glob of allegation? Will you table that histrionic
effrontery? Only a few gentle-people
have been granted the role

of defining
fries' maximum dangle. I do not stink from this
raspberry—I vacuum it. The enigmatic
filthy ocean will lip-synch, and

glue from that
fugue can lift the wall, and so my shallow courtesans,
rasp not what your bounty can glue
for you. Bask in what you

can prove true
at the boundary. My hollow criticisms whirl: mask not
what hysteria will accrue for you, but what
together we can stew for the freak

flag of RAM.
With gilded science our lonely ward, with mystery the
vinyl fudge of our weeds, let us reread
the sands above, asking this

dressing with
steady yelp, but showing that here in ether, gold's
worth must surely be harpooned.

Dream in the Headlights

She fell asleep
while driving in her sleep.

Routine medical
appointment? Unprecedented
weariness? The dream in

the dream did not surface.
Epilogue: she woke up while
waking up. Behind the wheel,

in unison with other highway
cars atop a tow truck.

MENACE IN HER DREAM

At 105, Coco escaped his bed
and reached mid-
Manhattan. He kept biting

couples heading
for their wedding

reception.
City Hall demanded

that you microwave him.
He resigned.

Post-Mortem Depression

Sometimes they make a mistake. Four or five
weeks ago, that's what happened.
I was there: I told them I wasn't
dead. Why should I kill myself? And then
we had to stumble through the thing again.

What are you going to do with the body? I don't
even know how the box opens.

Waiting Rheum

No one will be with you momentarily.
Neither a receptionist nor a professional pill
dispenser has gotten out of bed.

One scrawny soul
in a chair opposite becomes a flight canceled in

mid-air. Under enormous glasses, shaded to
prevent our seeing inside, a motionless centenarian
does not resist my removing them. I
encounter a box with another box inside: small

wooden eyes sitting there. If you can't find
water, look at the floor. There's a pedal.

Clutch

Don't purchase a bag
that doesn't close.
This
is New York City.

I'm sure it was a Jew
who invented zippers.

We don't need another
reason to be paranoid.

Construction

How are things going with the
building of the town? The name seems
woven to me. Jews were not allowed
to buy six apartments. We
couldn't catch the bruises.

This took so much more
paint than I thought it would. There might
be some chemical that melts
through. They throw things out
on the market red hot. Then it
freezes down before you can really
start to use them.

Everybody stops.
One big diamond.
All for nothing.
Nothing for all.

You twisted it. It's beginning to turn.

NOT A MARATHON

1952: we traded spontaneity
for solidarity.
Someone who would not speak

saw linen wrinkled.
Bathrooms never lie—
nor do urban
restaurants crawling with dybbuks.
I used him as I would use

any other liquid soap.
It wasn't the prospect of a marathon.

A Few Promises

A disco
for every
shut-in.

A bikini for every
introvert.

A staircase for
every stiletto.

A soft
wall for every
wallflower.

A tracking device for
Every tryst.

A
cherry atop
every libertine.

A straitjacket
for
every extrovert.

A casino in
every cortex.

A
prophet for every crapshoot.

A eulogy
for every
bride.

A condolence for every
milestone.

A monument
for
every snafu.

A chicken
in
every
warrior.

A
chicken
on every road.

Deep-fried chicken
before every gastric
by-pass.

A chicken
in every roast.

A pig in
every sty.

A frog
in
every kiss.

A rabbit under
every bed.

A window
in every dungeon.

A frozen dinner for
every loner.

Expiration
in every ambulance.

A blood donor
for every accident.

Aspirin for
every hopeless
aspirant.

An epidemic in
every
hypochondriac.

A
pageant
for every addiction.

A hairstylist in
every bald one.

A disease
for every medicine.

A Band-
aid for every
amputation.

A defibrillator for every
marathoner.

A cure for every
doctor.

A lawyer
for
every
litigant.

A suit
for every
lawyer.

A loophole
for every shyster.

A crackpot
behind
every jackpot.

A macramé freak
within every hedge
fund exec.

A rabid
vision inside
bureaucratic apathy.

A deluxe
condo for
every
noble fugitive.

A village for
every miscreant.

Unrequited
communion in every
logorrheic.

A mobile home
for every orangutan.

An honorary
doctorate in
every pole-
dancing
climate denier.

A Putin behind
every Twitter addict.

A lifetime achievement trophy
for
every bigot.

Hyperbole
in every anthem.

A fierce
opinion for every undecidable.

A loud
lout for
every
silent film.

An Oscar for
every depth plumber.

A poem for every
CPA.

Self-loathing
after every
credit card
massacre.

An heir
for every debtor.

A bank
in every oil
field.

A global death
drive in every megapolluter.

A pub
marathon
after
every
market plunge.

A manicure
for every
coal miner.

A banana
peel for every billionaire.

A thunderstorm for
every
carwash.

A forklift for
every grain.

A
strike
for
every blue collar.

A strike
in
every
bowler.

A splinter
in every chopstick.

A dimple in every wonton.

A thumb in every
pie.

A whisker
in every soup.

A diamond
in every
coffee cup.

A cupcake for
every dieter.

A queue
outside
every avocado warehouse.

An exercise video
for every
houseplant.

An umbrella
shielding
every black hole.

An
umbrella
in every
bathroom.

A bathtub
for every kitchen.

A
shark in every
bathtub.

A life
vest for
every
landsman.

A swimming pool
for every drought.

Ex-lax
for every
anal retentive.

A doorman in
every motor
home.

A sadist
within
every saint.

A knuckle for
every jawbone.

A
saint inside every sadist.

An executioner
for every housefly.

Absolution for
every do-
gooder.

A monster for every
swamp.

A scion
for every
psychotic.

A golden doodle
in every
pram.

A fairy
for
every tooth.

A pervert
for
every child.

A diamond in every
infant's ear.

A nonagenarian
in
every
newborn.

A pistol
in every school.

An underachiever
in every
classroom.

A
subway for
every
farmer.

A daydream in
every realist.

A cemetery
for every genius stroke.

A Martian
in
every earthling.

An earthling
in
every
Martian.

An
ocean for
every airplane.

A moustache
for every
meadow.

A book in every
cover.

A singer
in every library.

Acknowledgments

Blazevox: "Post-Mortem Depression"; "Homemaking"; "I Don't Want to See Her Damaged, So I'll Buy a New Pair of Glasses and Draw Her a New Face"; "I'm Bothering You, So Go Away"

ditch: "Waiting Rheum"

Marsh Hawk Review: "Almost Magnificent"; "Construction"; "Did They Dismiss School When Marilyn"; "Dream in the Headlights"; "Mirror"; "Not a Marathon"

Of(f)Course: "Corporate Angel"; "Gray Bus"

Otoliths: "Nothing New or Even Interesting"; "Remains"; "Sean and Dawn"; "Thanks, Mary"; "Weightlifter's Ghetto"; "You're Morally Inferior If"

Set: "Breathtakingly Dishonest"

About the Authors

A Pageant for Every Addiction is Thomas Fink's eleventh book of poetry. Recent collections include *Hedge Fund Certainty* (Meritage Press & i.e. Press, 2019) and *Selected Poems & Poetic Series* (Marsh Hawk Press, 2016). He has authored two books of criticism, including *A Different Sense of Power: Problems of Community in Late-Twentieth Century U.S. Poetry* (Fairleigh Dickinson University Press, 2001), and has co-edited two collections of criticism, including *Reading the Difficulties: Dialogues with Contemporary American Innovative Poetry* (University of Alabama Press, 2014). His poem, "Yinglish Strophes 9," was selected for *The Best American Poetry 2007* (Scribner's) by Heather McHugh and David Lehman. His paintings hang in various collections. Fink is Professor of English at City University of New York—LaGuardia.

Maya D. Mason, co-author with Thomas Fink of *Autopsy Turvy* (Meritage Press, 2010), has published in *BlazeVox*, *ditch*, *EOAGH*, *Helios Mss*, *Marsh Hawk Review*, *Offcourse*, and *Set*. She teaches fine art at various institutions, and her artwork is featured in various collections in New York and Europe.

TITLES FROM MARSH HAWK PRESS

Jane Augustine *Arbor Vitae; Krazy; Night Lights; A Woman's Guide to Mountain Climbing*

Tom Beckett *Dipstick (Diptych)*

Sigman Byrd *Under the Wanderer's Star*

Patricia Carlin *Original Green; Quantum Jitters; Second Nature*

Claudia Carlson *The Elephant House; My Chocolate Sarcophagus; Pocket Park*

Meredith Cole *Miniatures*

Jon Curley *Hybrid Moments; Scorch Marks*

Neil de la Flor *Almost Dorothy; An Elephant's Memory of Blizzards*

Chard deNiord *Sharp Golden Thorn*

Sharon Dolin *Serious Pink*

Steve Fellner *Blind Date with Cavafy; The Weary World Rejoices*

Thomas Fink *Selected Poems & Poetic Series; Joyride; Peace Conference; Clarity and Other Poems; After Taxes; Gossip*

Thomas Fink and Maya D. Mason *A Pageant for Every Addiction*

Norman Finkelstein *Inside the Ghost Factory; Passing Over*

Edward Foster *The Beginning of Sorrows; Dire Straits; Mahrem: Things Men Should Do for Men; Sewing the Wind; What He Ought to Know*

Paolo Javier *The Feeling is Actual*

Burt Kimmelman *Abandoned Angel; Somehow*

Burt Kimmelman and Fred Caruso *The Pond at Cape May Point*

Basil King *77 Beasts; Disparate Beasts; Mirage; The Spoken Word / The Painted Hand from Learning to Draw / A History*

Martha King *Imperfect Fit*

Phillip Lopate *At the End of the Day: Selected Poems and An Introductory Essay*

Mary Mackey *Breaking the Fever; The Jaguars That Prowl Our Dreams; Sugar Zone; Travelers With No Ticket Home*

Jason McCall *Dear Hero,*

Sandy McIntosh *The After-Death History of My Mother; Between Earth and Sky; Cemetery Chess; Ernesta, in the Style of the Flamenco; Forty-Nine Guaranteed Ways to Escape Death; A Hole In the Ocean; Lesser Lights; Obsessional*

Stephen Paul Miller *Any Lie You Tell Will Be the Truth; The Bee Flies in May; Fort Dad; Skinny Eighth Avenue; There's Only One God and You're Not It*

Daniel Morris *Blue Poles; Bryce Passage; Hit Play; If Not for the Courage*

Geoffrey O'Brien *The Blue Hill*

Sharon Olinka *The Good City*

Christina Olivares *No Map of the Earth Includes Stars*

Justin Petropoulos *Eminent Domain*

Paul Pines *Charlotte Songs; Divine Madness; Gathering Sparks; Last Call at the Tin Palace*

Jacquelyn Pope *Watermark*

George Quasha *Things Done for Themselves*

Karin Randolph *Either She Was*

Rochelle Ratner *Balancing Acts; Ben Casey Days; House and Home*

Michael Rerick *In Ways Impossible to Fold*

Corrine Robins *Facing It; One Thousand Years; Today's Menu*

Eileen R. Tabios *The Connoisseur of Alleys; I Take Thee, English, for My Beloved; The In(ter)vention of the Hay(na)ku; The Light Sang as It Left Your Eyes; Reproductions of the Empty Flagpole; Sun Stigmata; The Thorn Rosary*

Eileen R. Tabios and j/j hastain *The Relational Elations of Orphaned Algebra*

Susan Terris *Familiar Tense; Ghost of Yesterday; Natural Defenses*

Lynne Thompson *Fretwork*

Madeline Tiger *Birds of Sorrow and Joy*

Tana Jean Welch *Latest Volcano*

Harriet Zinnes *Drawing on the Wall; Light Light or the Curvature of the Earth; New and Selected Poems; Weather is Whether; Whither Nonstopping*

YEAR	AUTHOR	MHP POETRY PRIZE TITLE	JUDGE
2004	Jacquelyn Pope	*Watermark*	Marie Ponsot
2005	Sigman Byrd	*Under the Wanderer's Star*	Gerald Stern
2006	Steve Fellner	*Blind Date with Cavafy*	Denise Duhamel
2007	Karin Randolph	*Either She Was*	David Shapiro
2008	Michael Rerick	*In Ways Impossible to Fold*	Thylias Moss
2009	Neil de la Flor	*Almost Dorothy*	Forrest Gander
2010	Justin Petropoulos	*Eminent Domain*	Anne Waldman
2011	Meredith Cole	*Miniatures*	Alicia Ostriker
2012	Jason McCall	*Dear Hero,*	Cornelius Eady
2013	Tom Beckett	*Dipstick (Diptych)*	Charles Bernstein
2014	Christina Olivares	*No Map of the Earth Includes Stars*	Brenda Hillman
2015	Tana Jean Welch	*Latest Volcano*	Stephanie Strickland
2016	Robert Gibb	*After*	Mark Doty
2017	Geoffrey O'Brien	*The Blue Hill*	Meena Alexander
2018	Lynne Thompson	*Fretwork*	Jane Hirshfield
2019	Gail Newman	*Blood Memory*	Marge Piercy

ARTISTIC ADVISORY BOARD

For more information, please go to: www.marshhawkpress.org